LITTLE BIT O' NONSENSE ABOUT SHEEP

Compiled from the books of

Henry Brewis

Old Pond Publishing Ltd

First published 2008

ISBN 978-1-905523-97-9

Published by:
Old Pond Publishing Ltd
Dencora Business Centre
36 White House Road
Ipswich IP1 5LT
United Kingdom

www.oldpond.com

Compiled by Roger Smith
Book design by Liz Whatling
Printed and bound in Malta by Gutenberg Press Ltd

FOREWORD

'Tek the Huff' (or take the huff): a term used to describe a malady peculiar to sheep. The symptoms are a refusal to eat or move and, although a thorough veterinary examination may reveal no known disease or infection, the animal will expire when it's good and ready. Sometimes known as 'bloody awkwardness'.

These words of wisdom from Henry Brewis's book *Don't Laugh Till He's Out of Sight* just about sum up the Northumbrian author's attitude towards our woolly friends. In this compilation we have drawn on eight of his books to expand on this theme. Henry Brewis died in 2000. We trust he is looking benignly on this little bit o' nonsense from some other place where sheep come when called, shed their own coats and have eternal, worm-free lives – and pigs fly.

SOURCES

(numbers refer to page numbers in this book)

Clarts and Calamities: 6, 8, 10, 14, 20, 26, 28, 48, 54, 56, 58, 66, 72, 76, 78, 80. *Country Dance:* 12, 30, 70. *Chewing the Cud:* 49, 85, 86. *Don't Laugh Till He's Out of Sight:* 4, 22, 24, 34, 36, 38, 40, 42, 44, 46, 50, 52, 60, 64, 74, 84. *funnywayt'mekalivin':* 5, 11, 13, 16, 18, 25, 29, 31, 32, 35, 37, 41, 43, 45, 55, 59, 62, 63, 67, 81, 82, 83. *Goodbye Clartiehole:* 9, 17, 19, 23, 27, 53, 65, 71, 73, 77, 79. *Last Round-up:* 7. *The Magic Peasant:* 15, 21, 33, 39, 47, 51, 57, 61, 68, 69, 75, 87.

First get your sheep ...

For your first visit to a sheep sale you must carefully disguise yourself either as an impoverished idiot, recently released from an Old Shepherds' Rest Home, or as a dealer from Yorkshire, otherwise you will certainly be taken for a ride.

Even then you will inevitably end up with a couple of sheep who are stone blind, several consumed with footrot, eight with one tit, and a few broken-mouthed 'chasers' - all described by the auctioneer as "grand shiftin' gimmers off high ground".

"He says these sheep are from very high ground,
and they'll thrive anywhere!"

... then keep them in

The lambs I bought on Friday are of the 'homing' variety. They're rakers. No matter where I put the sods, they get out and immediately head in a westerly direction - consuming everything in their path like a plague of locusts. Already they've sampled the rape and the barley (which is just peeping through, and must've been amazed to find itself face to face with a ravenous cross-Suffolk hogg). They've been up the road into Charlie's barley as well, and into the village twice, eating the Pillicks' lawn and a few late-flowering shrubs. They're remarkable beasts. They can graze and run at the same time, which has to be bad for the digestion. They'll probably never get fat.

This morning they're back at the mart scratching about in the car park! I get them home before McMurdie sells them *again*.

"Never mind your glad tidings, mate – it'll take another bloody miracle to get my sheep back!"

Brought the two hoggs and their unexpected offspring into the croft.

At first I tried to simply walk them out of the gate, but of course all the rest went through quick as a flash, and I was left standing on the turnips with two hoggs, three lambs and Sweep.

Enter Willie, attracted by colourful language, and on to another plan. Put the lambs into the link box, and then catch the two hoggs.

Sweep gathered the whole lot into the corner, and Willie and I made a rush for one each. He caught his, but I missed the tackle, got trampled half t' death, and covered in clarts. Put Willie's victim into the link box (legs tied) and did the grabbing in the corner trick all over again. We were supposed to be going for the same hogg, but Willie got one and I got another. He got the right one.

He'll likely tell his mother about it.

"I must say, I always thought such language was confined to
Channel 4 after 9.30 p.m."

The yowes are still making a terrible row, primarily because six lambs have found their way home, and are trying to get into the hemmel. I briefly consider shooting the little buggers, but instead throw them into the pick-up and take them back to their mates. For a while I couldn't find where they'd escaped. The gate was still secure, and the fence is all pig netting down this side. Then I saw one of the six wanderers go straight to the water-trough. He was about to climb onto the ball-cock chamber and jump over the fence, but I just beat him to it, and felled him with m' stick. Two rails required - and a new stick.

"Sep, I think it's time you put your sheep inside during the winter."

They need feeding

There, dressed in pale blue overalls with a white lamb embroidered on the bib, pink wellies and woolly ski hat, Diana was trying to put some ewe nuts into the trough for her six mules. Not an impossible task you might think, but the sheep had become so excited at the prospect of nosh that they were continually barging in and knocking her down. The situation wasn't helped by the arrival of the three heifers, who naturally fancied a feed as well.

As he watched, she tried again … and, as soon as she lowered the bag, she was overwhelmed and thumped aside. A desperate battle ensued for the one protein nut that had rattled into the trough.

Again she tried (Geordie had to concede she was game). She was covered in clarts, tears running down her face, sobbing obscenities in a posh voice. "You barstards!" she cried. "Bugger orf!"

'Tomorrow," she said, "I may instruct Donald to shoot the whole bloody lot!"

"How many times have I told y' – for God's sake don't feed them till I've got a clear run to the gate!"

Feeding the yowes can be a time-consuming job - there's always at least one lame old bitch who takes an hour and a half to hobble to the troughs. The others are all there, waiting, ready for their nosh (probably been waiting all night) but old twinkle toes is at the far end of the field, of course.

There's one of these crippled creatures in both of the yow fields. I could put them into the croft with the tups, I suppose, but the rest would just draw lots to decide who should take their place - and the croft would be full in a week.

"It's the same every time he's had a night on the beer –
next morning we never get fed properly."

The shepherd

A peculiar breed is the shepherd
tending his flock to the end
you might think that he's wise when you look in his eyes
but in fact he's away round the bend.

He only believes what he wants to believe
nowt that he rears ever dies
and a night at the pub is no bloody good
if he cannot just sit tellin' lies.

There's just one who could tell y' the truth of course
how he strangled that champion mule hogg
how the tup met its fate when the lambing was late
and who shot that good collie dog.

Aye, his wife knows there's really no prospects
with a fella devoted to sheep
he'll rant and he'll rave from now to the grave
and shout, "Git away bye!" in his sleep....

"Don't look back, you fool ... they're gaining on y'!"

Hill farmer

Spare a thought for the man from oot bye
with his cap and his dog and his stick
through the sleet and the rain does he ever complain
if he didn't you'd think he was sick -

spare a thought for the man from the hill
where it's winter while spring at the coast
say a prayer for his cows and his poor blackie yowes
and his subsidy cheque in the post....

"Drugs, sex, violence, death…. I mean, what chance have we got when we grow up?"

Tupping

Sweep and I bring the hoggs into the pens, dose them (again), put them through the footbath (again) and move them onto the turnips. They only have a few drills to start with, till they get a taste for their new diet, but they fancy the leaves, and it's eyes down for a full bite.

I stay with them for a while, until they find the electric fence, have a sniff at it, get a shock and jump back. (Sweep knows all about electricity, and stays at the gate.) They look good, but if the weather breaks, they might need a run off onto a dry lie.

The tups have been out for a week now, and appear to be working alright, about a third of the 'girls' have blue bums.

"Not on yer life , Sonny. If you imagine I'm wandering around here
all winter covered in blue paint you must be mad!"

21

Sheepdogs are unnecessary

Collie dogs, often believed by beginners to be an essential part of the shepherd's equipment, are in fact both expensive and unnecessary. But if you insist on having a dog, then you'll have to learn to whistle with your mouth full of fingers, and swear at the same time.

The novice dog handler should stand in an exposed spot, staring enthusiastically into the middle-distance or in the general direction of some sheep and, holding his shepherd's stick in the right hand, shout in a loud clear voice such things as, "Git away bye!" or "Hadaway oot!" or "Cum inta m'shirt tail here!" or "For God's sake sit doon, y' donnered bugger!"

"I don't remember Clint Eastwood ever havin' this problem!"

A canny dog is the worst of all - he'll be totally inconsistent.

"Git away bye!" you'll shout on Monday morning, and off he'll go like a missile, fetch the flock nicely to hand and sit by your side eager for the next command, determined to please.

"Git away bye!" you'll say on Tuesday, and off he'll go like a missile - back home, leaving you screaming and pleading, threatening, foaming at the mouth, wishing you carried a gun.

"Git away bye!" you'll say on Wednesday - and he'll sit there looking as if you'd given the order in Swahili. Throw your stick at him and he'll probably pick it up and bury it.

Got the hoggs in off the turnips to draw a few out for tomorrow's mart. It took us all bleedin' morning!

It was Sweep's fault. He hasn't had much to do recently, and was full of himself, - wouldn't stop, went like a train, had the sheep running round in rings with me screaming for him to sit down. Of course, when we eventually got them to the gate he wouldn't let them out. Sat in the bloody gateway trying to look intelligent. I threw m' stick at 'im, some stones and m' hat. Then some of the hoggs bolted up the dyke. Sweep went in after them, so the main bunch stampeded through the gate and away up the road. A maniac in a car started blasting his horn at them, and about half of that group panicked through the hedge in amongst some yowes.

Now we had some on the road, some others in the wrong field being chatted up by a tired tup, and the rest still on the turnips. It took until dinner time to get them all together again and into the pens.

"Wottya makin' all the fuss about ... you're on the wrong road, anyway!"

Shearing – a man's job

I remember m' father was a useful clipper. He would just stroll into the catching pen and grab the first sheep t' hand, no looking for bare bellies - they were all the same t' him.

Once he'd got the yow cowped, he'd give it a right good hammerin' and more or less render it unconscious. Then while it was in a sort of coma he'd have the fleece off in three minutes flat.

"D' y' fancy your kiss of life trick again, Charlie?"

They all came to watch the clipping, pointing and giggling as naked yowes ran off bleating for their lambs, leaving a pile of wool behind. They were impressed how quickly Willie and his mate Alfie could disrobe a sheep.

Alfie was built to resemble a small byre. He moved like a combination of John Wayne and Terminator 2, handled yowes as if they were paper bags, and swore with a vocabulary that was unfamiliar to Prudence. When a lean, fidgety beast with no rise presented a few problems, and eventually left with several bits missing, followed by some colourful language - the audience began to mutter and shuffle. When Alfie removed half a lug from another awkward sheep there was blood everywhere; the plumber's wife from No.3 fainted and had to be helped home for a brandy.

"This must be another one y' clipped last year, Charlie – its lugs are missin'"

The clipper

The first one had no rise at all
sticky tight and full of grease
backbone like a railway line
kicked and wriggled all the time
couldn't wrap the fleece.

Picked a belly bare and smooth
a gimmer young and fit
clippers hummin' like a song
no sooner started she was gone
minus half a tit.

Horny mule easy caught
like handles on a jug
stupid bitch was seven crop
I thought the blood would never stop
cut off her near-side lug.

Got a nervous twitchin' thing
who jumped about wild-eyed
she left me sittin' on the floor
trousers ripped and then what's more
she lay quite still and died!

"For God's sake don't switch off, Charlie –
you've only got about thirty seconds t' clip this one."

So with the rest of the club looking on, together with a few parents and a judge, half a dozen of us grabbed a sheep each and prepared to impress the gallery.

"Are you all ready?" said the judge. "Go!"

I'd no sooner got mine 'opened up' around the neck, than I realised to my dismay she had one of her horns fast in my flies, and as I paused momentarily to consider the implications of this, she went away. She just got up and went away - taking with her a substantial and important section of my trousers.

Farming's like that - it's never easy to hide your inadequacies.

"Never mind, Son. Rome wasn't built in a day, y' know."

If Sep has been stacking straw bales all day, he stacks straw bales all night as well. He whips his wife's pillow out from under her and stacks it on top of his, - then whips his pillow out and stacks it on top of hers. And so on - and so on - all night - until they get up, exhausted.

It's even worse if he's been clipping sheep - he has the nightie off her half a dozen times, and wrapped up!

Lambing – time to go insane

Firstly then a few tips for the lambing season.

Contrary to most learned works on the subject, I believe it to be inadvisable to feed the pregnant ewe more than the absolute minimum for survival. This enables you to achieve the desired emaciated flock which, when the necessity arises, you'll find much easier to catch. (A word of warning here - it can be dangerous at this stage to make a noise like a bale of hay, as you will run the risk of being overwhelmed before you can climb out over the gate.)

Avoid at all costs the time-wasting practice of erecting straw-bale shelters, because you will find that on a particularly stormy night the ewes will either lie on the windward side and perish, or eat the straw bales - and then perish.

"We could be in trouble, girls. The man's a nervous wreck –
you'd think he'd never done a lambin' in his life before."

It is imperative that the new shepherd fully understands the ewe's attitude at this time. Her first priority is of course to die, and failing that she believes her only real hope for salvation in the hereafter is to ensure that the shepherd dies - or at least becomes a gibbering wreck estranged from his wife and family.

Extreme care must be taken when the ewe actually gives birth to her offspring. One must remember that sheep are unable to count accurately above nought - consequently although on occasions she may be aware of motherhood, she will be unsure as to what extent, and could well abandon one or all of her lambs, pretending she was elsewhere at the time. She may just as readily claim everybody else's.

"Now, girls, it'll soon be lambing time again. We'll have to decide who's to have the privilege of suddenly dropping dead for no apparent reason."

Pet lamb

He was born alone and friendless
on a wet'n windy night
and his mother died unaided
apparently from fright –
so we fed him on the bottle
as he piddled on the mat
which soon upset the Labrador
and prop'ly huffed the cat.

But he lived somewhat reluctant
sucking everything in sight
ate herbaceous borders
and bleated half the night –
we kicked him and we cursed him
always scratchin' at the door
the postie ran him over twice,
he still came back for more.

Pot-bellied and peculiar
he just refused to grow
a hungry little nuisance
till the time he had to go –
by the winter he looked better
eating turnips, nuts and hay,
but he crept into the grain store
and blew up on Christmas Day!

"Quick as y' can, Vicar. We've got a yow lambin' – "

A stout net-stake is also very useful when 'setting–on' the orphan lamb. More often than not, the ewe, elated at having lost her own young ones, refuses to be lumbered with somebody else's hungry brat, but her mind (I use the word advisedly), can be 'changed', if she is first rendered semi-conscious by the above-mentioned lambing aid. Golf enthusiasts have discovered that a 7 iron has a similar effect.

"Just a little bit further, Son – then I'll show y' how to persuade the ewe t' take the other lamb."

"Had a good lambin'?" asks this bloke at the mart.

"Well, canny, y' know - not bad."

"Aye, heard y' had some bother wi' them South Country hoggs y' bought." He was smiling already.

"Well they were a bit wild, took some handling."

"We heard y' couldn't catch them." He was giggling now.

"Yes, they were a bit flighty," I said.

"They tell me only half of them lambed." There were tears rolling down his face, and he was nudging the fella standing next to him, who was laughing quite openly. "You should've stuck with the mules, son."

"You're probably right," I said weakly.

"Oh, it's right enough." He was wiping his eyes and pulling himself together. "We had a grand lambin'; those old yowes just lamb themselves y' know - never any bother."

" ... and I get the impression the lambin's not goin' too well, either."

Not a good day. We have a yow with mastitis. It took me twenty minutes to catch the creature, by which time I was on the brink of a cardiac (again). Tied her legs together with a piece of baler twine, wrapped m' anorak around her head, and went home for penicillin and syringe. When I got back, the other yowes, presumably thinking my coat to be a bag of protein pellets, had dragged it off, and eaten half of it. However, madam was still there. She was injected and marked for future reference.

It was nine o'clock before I got to the last field, and here I found another yow on her back in a rig bottom. She'd obviously been there all night, and was very wobbly. Another hour or so, and she'd have been a gonna. It took her quite a while to have a pee and stagger off. Her lambs had little sympathy - all they were interested in was breakfast, and they attacked the poor thing like a pair of piranhas.

"Remember all that fuss about overworked doctors falling asleep during delicate operations?"

Let me tell you that the Cheviot hogg is especially designed to induce premature heart problems. You've gotta get up very early to get the better of those creatures. They travel at the speed of light, propelled by a constantly revolving tail - with a demented gleam in their eye, a total lack of maternal instinct, and a conviction that the shepherd is out to slaughter them all.

By the time I'd finished lambin' two hundred of them, they weren't far wrong. I was a decade older and speaking to nobody.

But that was just the beginning. No sooner had they been dealt with, than the main flock of half-breds came in. They were enormous walking billiard tables, who lived only to eat.

They were a lot slower, easier to catch (harder to cowp), but still with that inbred talent to drop dead for no apparent reason - they would limp about with their 'back-body' sticking out like the brake lights on a motor bike, and produce triplets while firing on one tit. It was quite a normal lambin' with them, I suppose.

"Mother, do I *have* t' be a farmer when I grow up?"

For example, after the most disastrous lambing in years, during which half the yowes are geld and the other half abort, the tup is shot, and the collie dog runs away with a lurcher - the peasant must be able to rid his mind of these sordid little details, take a deep breath and talk in terms of 'a canny lambin' regardless.

If not, he can become suicidal or crackers within weeks.

"Yes, I think we must assume the last yow has finally lambed, now!"

Dipping

The water is almost freezing. Some of our more mature ladies wouldn't survive for more than ten seconds in the tub, and they know it. The stubborn auld buggers resist all attempts to push them towards the drop, digging their toes into the slightest crack in the cement. It's a battle with every yow. Occasionally one will fool you by doing the running jump trick, and only falls from flight onto another unfortunate yow below, who is paddling gamely for the steps and survival.

There's a lot of colourful language. Gordon has a vast vocabulary, and I think Willie's is substantially enlarged by the end of the operation.

We have them all through by one o'clock. Gordon and I are cold, wet and miserable, and I expect the sheep are too, but Willie swallows a bacon sandwich, and hurries off to play rugby. If he handles the opposition like he handles yowes, he could be sent off today.

"Got 'im on a job creation scheme – I think he's been one of them SAS blokes!"

Today is sheep's feet day, everything gets a pedicure. The lambs have scald, the yowes have outgrowing toe nails, even the tups are limping about like wounded soldiers. Charlie calls in, and he's limping too - a cow stood on his foot.

Getting the flock through the footbath is a swearing, punching, kicking, spitting, stick-waving pantomime. The lambs won't go unless hurled bodily into the bath. The yowes either stand stubbornly refusing to budge, or leap the whole length of the trough. I drag one old mule through, hoping a few will follow, but no luck. I grab another awkward bitch, pull her half-way and am immediately overwhelmed by the rest of her mates. By the end of the operation I'm suffocated by fumes, covered in muck, eyes and nose streaming ... and limping with a wonky knee.

"Good idea, isn't it?"

Lambs scoured t' death in South field, several not 'doing' at all. Got them in and dosed the lot with the latest wonder worm drench, and beat them (and their bloody-minded mothers) through the footbath as well. As usual they either fly through, tip-toeing over the water, or they stand with their front feet in the trough, and refuse to move any further.

That foot-rot stuff always makes my eyes water, and by the end of the job they were red, and I was coughing and splutterin' like a calf with husk.

Gladys says she's not impressed with my aroma either.

"C'mon girls, it's lovely. Really!"

Worms

It is worth noting also that sheep are life-long members of the 'worm benevolent society', and as such do everything in their power to provide a suitable comfy home for all species of parasitic organisms, from ticks to nematodirus. A sheep is actually a worm in sheep's clothing! (Not many people know that.)

"Whoops. Sorry, Charlie."

The vet

She got a tin of Terramycin
and a bottleful of dope,
a pint of penicillin
and a canny bit of hope.

The vet was optimistic -
he'd worked miracles before -
but the yow was quite determined
and she died at half past four.

The vet was very sad indeed,
he thought it might've lived
and I was disappointed too
'cos he charged me thirty quid.

"It's fluke," said the vet. "Yes, fluke, that's what it is alright, no doubt about it. Or possibly pulpy kidney, yes it could be pulpy kidney … unless of course it's a cobalt deficiency, there's a lot of that about just now …or staggers perhaps - that's what it'll be, staggers. Then again, mind you, it might be foot and mouth, or even fowl pest - you can never be too sure with mule ewes y' know. But fear not, we'll soon have her up and about again, good as new."

He gave the sheep fourteen injections, a gallon of drench, thirty-eight bright yellow pills, covered her feet with Stockholm tar, wrapped a hot bran poultice round her head, and drove off in his big car singing, "It's the rich what get the pleasure and the poor what get the blame."

"Look, I've invented the wheel. It could revolutionise the treatment of lame yowes!"

A sheep's ambition is to die ...

We have a yow looking very depressed. I quickly deduce that this is not the result of frustrated motherhood, but rather one of the many obscure and incurable afflictions peculiar to sheep. The symptoms are as follows: head down, lugs droopy, slavering, glazed look in the eyes, wobbly gait. However, when I try to catch the creature to dose it with Robbie's patent elixir, it bolts off leaving me clutching a handful of wool, and runs at great speed into the tree. This is not a happy sheep.

"Y' knew he was comin', didn't y'!"

Mary had a little lamb
I'm glad it wasn't mine
cos' its fleece came out in handfuls
and it suffered from the pine.

Mary stuffed it full of cobalt
and a dose of copper neat
which didn't cure the shot-jaw
or the rotten scalded feet.

It also got pneumonia
and staggers in the spring
it couldn't even run away
the knackered brainless thing.

It hung about for ages
and then it broke her heart
when it dropped down dead last Wednesday
in the ring at Hexham Mart.

"She's not goin' t' wake up, Son. She's achieved her life's ambition now."

The sheep men still wander in with that bewildered expression sheep men often have, talk wistfully of days when the Ministry sent a cheque after every mart, and compare improbable tales of death among their flocks.

"Y'll never believe this," says Willie, "but we had a lamb ate a mole trap last week. Found it dead as a maggot with the trap stuck in his throat … choked t' death … a right good lamb 'n' all!"

"That's nowt," declares Charlie, unimpressed . "Y' know the chain on a hay heck … it has a hook on the end t' fasten down the lid - know what I mean? Well, we had a lamb swallowed the hook … like a bloody suicidal salmon. There it was, stone dead yesterday mornin'!"

"So, who said there's no such thing as a free lunch … eh?"

It's a bright morning as I walk out to inspect the stock and, surprise, surprise, I come across a recently deceased lamb. And no, it's not the rubbishy little crit I half-expected to snuff it, it's not the one who's been scoured skinny since birth, nor that pathetic triplet that's never had a decent suck since he was born.

It is of course a superb creature who was destined for the mart next week. The sod!

"Inland revenue, bank statement, four bills, a final demand,
no subsidy cheque ... and you've got a dead lamb in the bottom field."

The yow is a truly remarkable beast
that man's been unable to tame
she would never be caught if God hadn't thought
to make most of the stupid things lame.

The auld yow is born a peculiar beast
she defies mother nature's great plan
no creature on earth has ambition at birth
to drop dead just as soon as she can.

The yow is a thoroughly awkward beast
from her lugs to the tip of her tail
two tits and a tooth and t' tell you the truth
a brain like a mouldy straw bale!

"I wouldn't, if I was you, Tommy. I'm not sure he's
in the right frame of mind for it."

At breakfast time a wagon comes for the wool, and Charlie phones to say he's got twenty yowes and lambs belonging to me in his hayfield. Sweep and I go to bring them back, and one of the yowes collapses half-way down the road. She won't get up, so I have to leave her there.

When I go back with the pickup to collect the old bitch, she's grazing on the roadside, and I have a hell of a job catching her. There I was kicking her into the pickup, telling her what I thought of her in simple peasant language, when the Reverend cycles past, all sweetness and light.

"... Morning," he says chirpily, and quotes something about the one that went astray. (Does he mean the yow or me?)

"Don't be ridiculous. That won't work ... she's been dead since Tuesday!"

Off to the mart

One of the lambs in the croft, drawn out ready for the mart, a prime animal, a superb beast in every way, as fit as a lintie yesterday - is lying deceased! Stiff!

I am very upset, and jump up and down on the carcass, screaming every obscenity I can remember from an extensive rural vocabulary. This confirms Gladys's opinion that she married a maniac - but fails to revive the lamb!

Of the remainder, one is rejected. How can he reject a good healthy lamb of twenty kilos taken straight from his mother? The tup staggers through this last ordeal, and raises ten quids' worth of sympathy.

"I believe you, madam. A very rare breed indeed. But unfortunately so is the peasant farmer willing to give you a bid for it."

The lambs made 4p a kilo less than the national average for last week, and two were rejected. Arthur Thompson has about a dozen rejected every week. He just leaves them on the old railway line behind the mart, and presents them to Ghadaffi a week later. Sometimes it works, sometimes it doesn't. He currently has fifty running about on the embankment, eating cinders and weeds in the hope that they'll become thin enough to grade.

Well, you'd be huffed as well, if y' thought *that's* all y' were worth."

The ministry grader

Three cheers for the Ministry Grader
he's a charming and lovable bloke
so get down on your knees
say thank you and please
and remember to laugh at his jokes.

Hats off to the Mart Ayatollah
always be humble and meek
he's knocked three kilos off
but the man's still a toff -
he could nicely reject them next week!

It was a Friday, and Sep had sold a few sheep at the mart. The lambs made a fair enough trade - but the highlight had been the achievement (it was nothing less), of persuading two geriatric mule yowes actually to walk into the ring unaided. What's more they managed to stay upright until they were sold and minutes later the pair staggered out again (coughing in perfect harmony), and Sep found himself twenty quid richer than he had any right to expect.

Perhaps it was the euphoria of this minor miracle, but he made his first mistake when he got home - he told Gladys about it. She said nowt, but she had the twenty pounds 'spent' before the kettle boiled.

"C'mon, Sep. It's no use – she's a gonna!"

Dying race

The yow is a creature I've studied too long
and still found no reason to burst into song
the beast is not witty, amusing, well read
and gives the impression she'd rather be dead.

They're awkward, they're brainless, you must come to terms
that bugs and bacteria and most of all worms
will assist every sheep to escape from this earth
as quickly as possible soon after birth.

The breed doesn't matter, they're all on a par,
the trouble comes with them you needn't look far,
their only appeal comes much later of course
with small new potatoes and tasty mint sauce.

"Who said sheep rustlin' was easy money?
For God's sake let's stick t' robbin' banks from now on."

HENRY BREWIS

Born near Alnwick, Northumberland in 1932, Henry Brewis was one of a clan of farmers in the area. He spent much of his life running a mixed arable and livestock farm at Hartburn, near Morpeth, Northumberland.

In the 1970s he began drawing cartoons and writing regularly for farming magazines, including the *West Cumberland Farmers Journal*, regional NFU journals and *Livestock Farming*. His first full collection of cartoons, *funnnywayt'mekalivin'*, was published in 1983, following which Henry gave up farming to become a full-time writer and illustrator.

Titles by Henry Brewis currently in print
and available from Old Pond Publishing include:

Cartoon books	**Stories and verses**	**Audio CDs**
Chewing the Cud	*Clarts and Calamities*	*Rural Stew and*
Funnywayt'mekalivin'	*Country Dance*	*Country Casserole*
Last Round-up	*Don't Laugh Till He's Out of Sight*	*Shepherd's Pie*
The Magic Peasant	*Harvey and the Handy Lads* (children's)	
	Night Shift	

www.oldpond.com